For children

This book is just like *Far Out, Brussel Sprout!* — it's full of rhymes, riddles, jokes and games that come from, and belong to, all the children of Australia. So many children wrote to me and sent me their favourite rhymes I knew we had to have another book. Here it is!

My thanks to everyone who wrote. I've tried to answer all the letters, but I think this book is the best 'answer' I could give. It's not just a book *for* children, it's a book *by* children. It belongs to you because you (together with all the other children) made it. But you shouldn't be surprised if some of the grown-ups you know enjoy it too. Don't forget — even the oldest person was a child once.

My address is at the bottom of this page, and I'd be pleased to hear from you. You could write and tell me of the games you play, the rhymes, riddles and jokes you know. Perhaps some of you would like to send drawings of children playing. Who knows, maybe we'll be able to make another book together!

June Factor

June Factor
Institute of Early Childhood Development
Madden Grove
Kew Victoria 3101

Acknowledgements

Some of the material in this book comes from the Australian Children's Folklore Collection, an archive of children's lore housed in the Institute of Early Childhood Development, Melbourne. Most of the rhymes and chants were sent to me by children, and by adults who remembered the pleasures of their own childhood. My grateful thanks to them all, and to Gwenda Davey, Darryn Kruse and Barbara McKenzie for their assistance.

This book is dedicated to all the

Gretas
Isabels
Ruths
Lians
Sonias

and

Brankos
Owens
Yiannis and
Sams

of Australia

ALL RIGHT, VEGEMITE!

A new collection of Australian children's chants and rhymes

Compiled by June Factor
Illustrated by Peter Viska

Melbourne
Oxford University Press
Oxford Auckland New York

OXFORD UNIVERSITY PRESS AUSTRALIA

Oxford New York Toronto
Delhi Bombay Calcutta Madras Karachi
Petaling Jaya Singapore Hong Kong Tokyo
Nairobi Dar es Salaam Cape Town
Melbourne Auckland
and associated companies in
Beirut Berlin Ibadan Nicosia

OXFORD is a trademark of Oxford University Press.

VEGEMITE is a registered trademark of Kraft Foods Limited.

© This collection June Factor 1985
© Illustrations Peter Viska 1985
First published 1985
Reprinted 1986 four times, 1987 three times

This book is copyright. Apart from any fair
dealing for the purposes of private study,
research, criticism or review as permitted under
the Copyright Act, no part may be reproduced,
stored in a retrieval system, or transmitted, in
any form or by any means electronic, mechanical,
photocopying, recording, or otherwise without
prior written permission. Inquiries should be
made to Oxford University Press.

National Library of Australia
Cataloguing-in-Publication data:

All right, Vegemite (A new collection of Australian children's
   chants and rhymes).

For children.
ISBN 0 19 554664 4.

1. Counting-out rhymes — Australia. 2. Folk-lore
   and children — Australia. I. Factor, June. II. Viska, Peter

398'.8'0994

Typeset by Bookset, Melbourne
Printed in Australia by Impact Printing, Melbourne
Published by Oxford University Press, 253-273 Normanby Road,
   South Melbourne, Australia

Blessed is he who sitteth on an ant hill
For he shall surely rise.

Sweet little Emily Rose
Sat on a chair to pose,
But young brother Jack
On that chair put a tack —
And sweet little Emily . . . rose!

Mary the milk maid
Was milking the cow,
The trouble with Mary
She didn't know how.
Along came the farmer
And gave her the sack,
So she turned the cow over
And poured the milk back!

A little birdie from on high
Dropped a message from the sky.
As I wiped it from my eye
I thanked the Lord that cows don't fly.

In jail you get coffee
In jail you get tea
In jail you get everything
Except the jailhouse key.

Dictation, dictation, dictation,
A man had a big operation.
They pulled out his gizzards
And thought they were lizards,
Dictation, dictation, dictation.

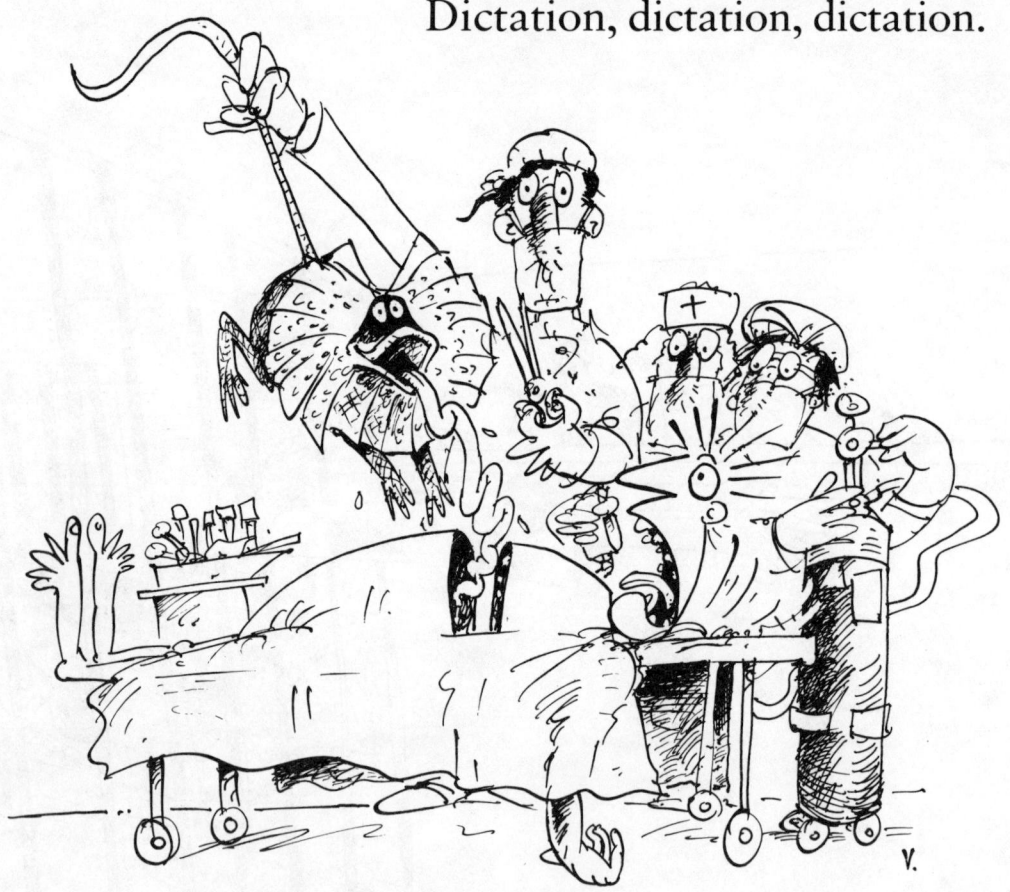

Dictation, dictation, dictation,
Three sausages went to the station.
One got lost,
One squashed,
The other had a big operation.

All right, Vegemite!

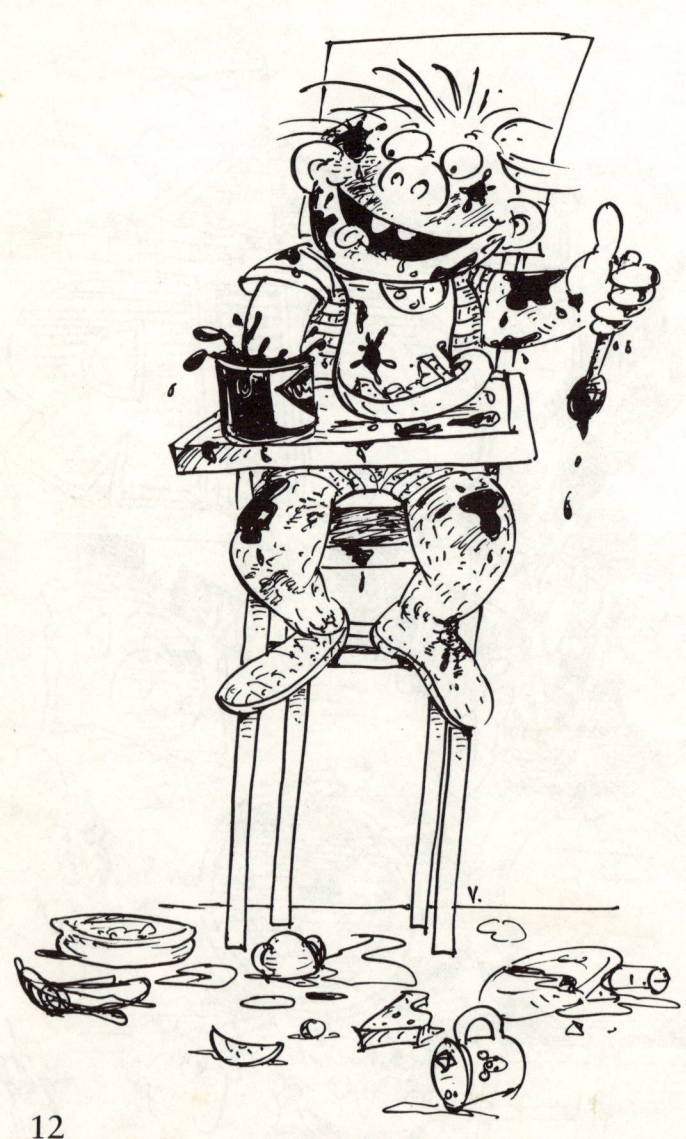

Jelly belly custard, pizza pie,
All mixed together with a dead-dog's eye.
Slam it on a pancake, nice and thick,
Then eat it all up with a cup of sick.

Little Robin Red-Breast
Sat upon a thistle,
Every time he wagged his tail
He gave a little whistle.

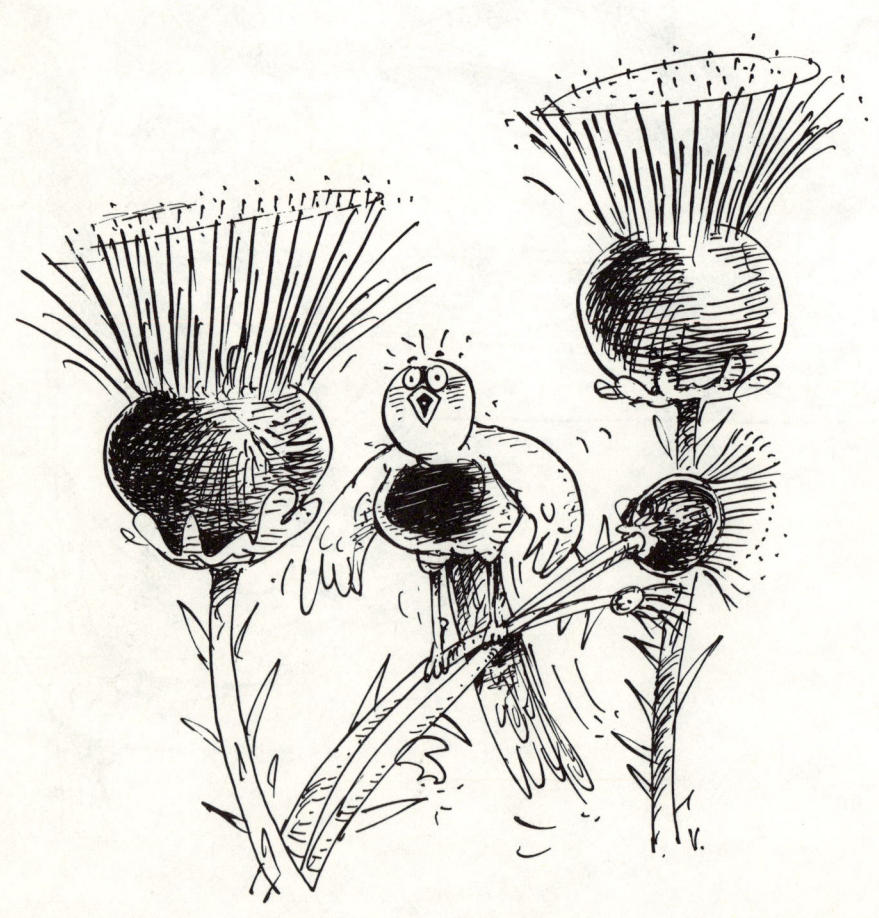

I'm Popeye the sailor man,
I live in a garbage can,
I eat all the worms
And spit out the germs,
I'm Popeye the sailor man.

Erky Perky was a worm,
A little worm was he,
He sat upon the railway track
The train he did not see.
Erky Perky!

The boy stood on the burning deck
Picking his nose like mad.
He rolled it in to little balls
And threw them at his dad.

Nobody likes me, everybody hates me,
I think I'll go and eat some worms.
Big ones, small ones,
Fat ones, skinny ones,
Worms that squiggle and squirm.
Bite their heads off,
Suck their blood out,
Throw their skins away.
Nobody knows how much I like 'em —
I eat 'em three times a day.

Great big lumps of
Greasy grimy gopher guts
Marinated monkey meat
Little piggies' hairy feet
All mixed up with
Percolated porpoise pus.
AND I FORGOT MY SPOON!

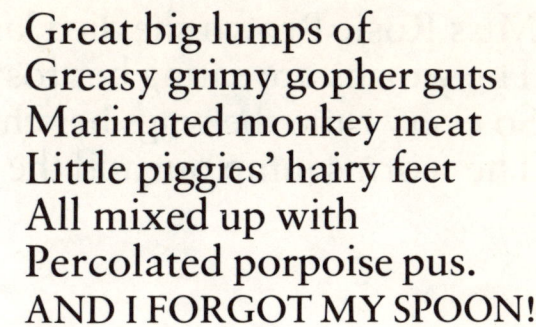

Miss Rosie Brown she died last week,
The worms are eating her rosy cheek;
So every time she wags her chin
The worms jump out and the worms jump in.

Billy Smith is no good,
Chop him up for firewood.
If he is no good for that
Give him to the old tomcat!

I had a little dog,
His name was Tim,
I put him in the bathtub
To see if he could swim.
He drank all the water,
He ate all the soap,
I took him to the doctor,
The doctor said, 'No hope.'

I love my teddy bear,
Blue eyes and curly hair.
Put him in a salmon tin
Squash his little tummy in.
I love my teddy bear!

Harry had a guillotine
And tried it out on sister Jane.
Said Mother as she got the mop,
'These messy games have got to stop.'

There once was a bird called Fat,
Who started to eat up a cat.
His mother said, 'Hey!'
And threw it away,
'Eat someone your own size, you brat.'

Willie in one of his bright blue sashes
Fell in the fire and was burnt to ashes.
Mother said, 'Though the room grows chilly,
I haven't the heart to poke poor Willy.'

There's music in a horseshoe,
There's music in a nail,
There's music in a tomcat
If you only pull his tail.

It was a cold and wintry night,
A man stood in the street,
His aged eyes were full of tears
And his boots were full of feet.

It's hard enough to find a friend,
It's hard to find a hope,
But it's harder still to find a towel
When your eyes are full of soap.

Ducks in the long grass,
Quack, quack, quack.
Lovers in the long grass —
Smack, smack, smack.

Two lovers walked along the beach,
They held each other's hands,
Their hearts were full of tender love,
Their shoes were full of sand.

Pop goes the bottle,
Pop goes the cider,
Mum pops into bed
And Pop pops in beside her.

Here comes the bride,
All dressed in white,
Slipped on a banana skin
And went for a ride!

I love you, I love you, I love you almighty,
I wish your pyjamas were next to my nightie.
Now don't be mistaken,
Now don't be misled,
I mean on the clothesline
And not in the bed.

If you build a better mousetrap
And put it in your house,
Before long Mother Nature
Will build a better mouse.

Mother's in the kitchen
Cooking fish and chips,
Father's in the toilet
Bombing battle ships!

A doctor fell into a well
And broke his collar-bone.
A doctor should attend the sick
And leave the well alone.

Australia is a free land,
Free without a doubt —
If you haven't any dinner
Then you're free to go without.

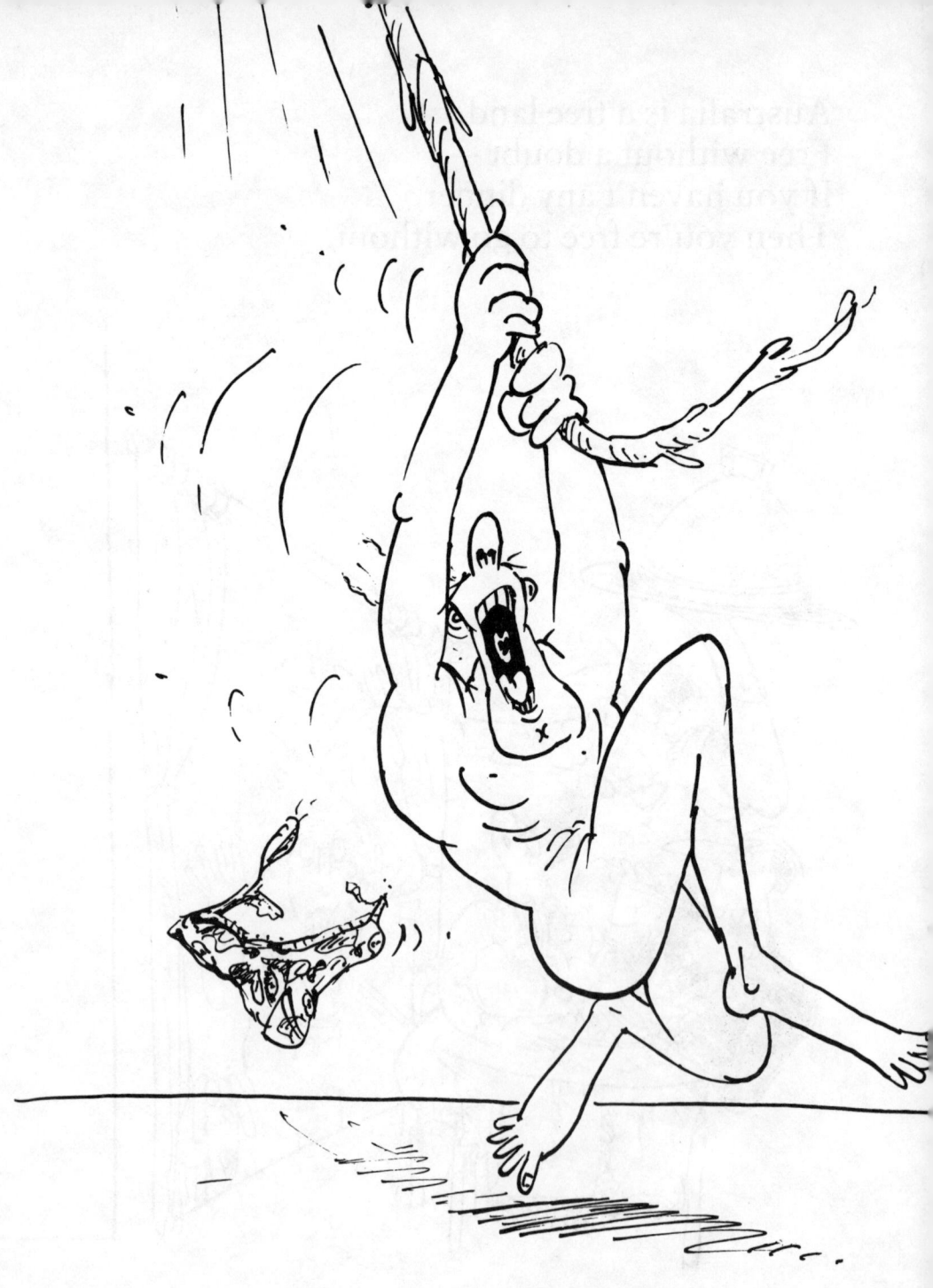

Teacher, teacher, don't be dumb,
Give me back my bubble gum.
Teacher, teacher, don't be mean,
Give me a coin for the coffee machine.
Teacher, teacher, I declare —
Tarzan's lost his underwear!

Algy saw the bear.
The bear saw Algy.
The bear was bulgy.
The bulge was Algy.

Car in the ditch
Man in the tree
Moon was full
And so was he.

See you later, chip potata.

See you round like a rissole.

Real cool, swimming pool!

Real keen, baked bean!

Fuzzy-wuzzy was a bear,
Fuzzy-wuzzy had no hair.
If Fuzzy-wuzzy had no hair
He wasn't fuzzy-wuzzy.

Dan, Dan, the dunny man,
Washed his face in the frying pan,
Combed his hair
With the leg of a chair
And told his mother he didn't care.

The elephant is a graceful bird,
It flies from bough to bough,
It makes a nest in a rhubarb tree
And whistles like a cow.

Sam, Sam, the dirty man,
Washed his face in a frying pan,
He combed his hair with a donkey's tail
And scratched his belly with a big toe nail.

There was a young man from Perth,
Who was born on the day of his birth.
He was married they say
On his wife's wedding day
And died on his last day on earth.

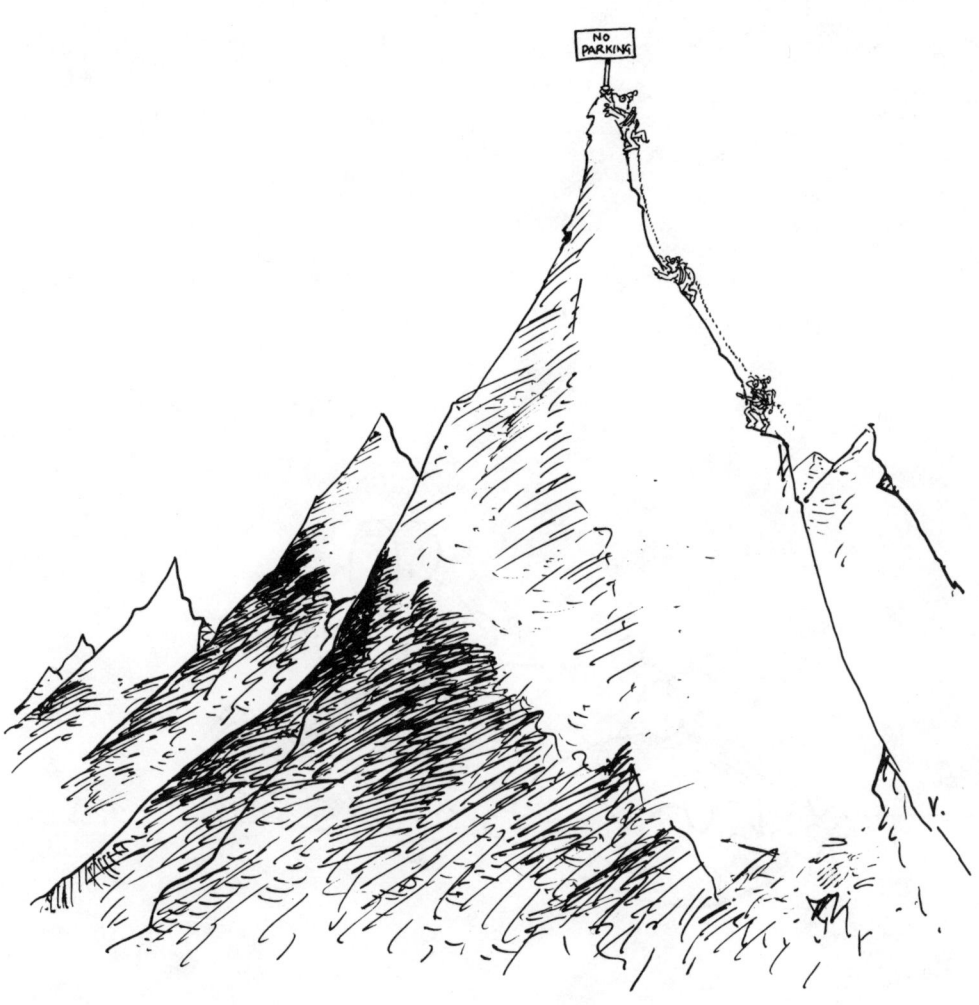

If you notice this notice,
You'll notice this notice
Is not worth noticing.

Any noise annoys an oyster,
But a noisy noise annoys an oyster more.

A tutor who tooted the flute
Tried to tutor two tooters to toot.
Said the two to the tutor,
'Is it harder to toot, or
To tutor two tooters to toot?'

Old Mother Hubbard
Went to her cupboard
To fetch her poor dog a bone.
When she got there
Her cupboard was bare
So the poor little dog had Pal.

Old Mother Hubbard
Went to the cupboard
To get her poor daughter a dress.
When she got there
The cupboard was bare
And so was her daughter, I guess.

Twinkle, twinkle little star,
How I wonder what you are,
Up above the world so high,
Eating steak and kidney pie.
Twinkle, twinkle little star,
How I wonder what you are.

Twinkle, twinkle little star,
How I wonder what you are,
Up above the world so high
Like a diamond in the sky.
Don't you know, my little mite,
I'm really a RUSSIAN SATELLITE!

Twinkle, twinkle little star,
Like an onion in a jar,
Never sit on a nest of ants
Unless you're wearing cast-iron pants.

Humpty Dumpty sat on a wall,
Humpty Dumpty had a great fall.
All the King's horses and all the King's men
Had fried eggs and bacon for breakfast again.

Humpty Dumpty sat on the wall,
Humpty Dumpty had a great fall.
All the King's horses and all the King's men
Said, 'Oh no, not scrambled eggs again!'

Roses are red,
Violets are blue,
Smelly socks
Remind me of you.

Roses are red,
Coal is black,
Do me a favour,
Go sit on a tack.

The roses have faded,
The violets are dead,
The sugar bowl's empty
And so is your head.

Roses are red,
Violets are blue,
The back of the bus
Reminds me of you.

Mary had a little lamb,
The lamb was very tough.
And in the circumstances
A little was enough.

Mary had a little lamb,
Her brother had some chicken,
And so betwixt them both you see
They did some finger lickin'.

Mary had a little lamb,
A little pork, a little ham,
An ice-cream then some soda fizz,
And boy — how sick our Mary is!

Mary had a little lamb,
It had a touch of colic,
She fed it brandy twice a day
And now it's alcoholic.

Mary had a wristlet watch,
She swallowed it one day,
And now she's taking Beecham's pills
To pass the time away.

Mary had a little lamb,
You've heard this tale before,
But did you know she passed her plate
And had a little more?

Mary had a little lamb,
An intellectual nit,
It never passed its first exam
Because it couldn't sit!

Charlie Chaplin sat on a pin.
How many inches did it go in?
1, 2, 3 . . .

Don't be mistaken
Don't be in doubt
I didn't see you getting in
I saw you climbing out.

I saw you in the ocean
I saw you in the sea
I saw you in the bathtub —
Whoops! Pardon me!

I ackey chew tobaccy,
I ackey out.
If you had been where I had been
You wouldn't have been counted out.

Ellery bellery ripperty rah,
Ripperty rah terollar,
Every man who has no beard
Ought to wear a collar.

Hicketty, picketty, high silicketty,
Pompalairy jig,
Every man who has no hair
Ought to wear a wig.

My boyfriend's name is Tony
He came from Macaroni
With twenty-four toes
And a pickle on his nose
And this is how my story goes:
One day when I was walking
I heard my boyfriend talking
To a pretty little girl
With a strawberry curl
He jumped in the lake
And swallowed a snake
And came back out with a belly-ache.
I hate to scrub the dishes
I hate to scrub the floor
But I love to kiss my boyfriend
Behind the kitchen door door door.

My boyfriend gave me an apple,
My boyfriend gave me a pear,
My boyfriend gave me a kiss on the lips
And threw me down the stairs.

I gave him back the apple,
I gave him back the pear,
I gave him back the kiss on the lips
And threw him down the stairs.

My young man has gone to France
To teach the ladies how to dance,
When he comes back
He'll marry me
We'll dance the konker
One, two, three.

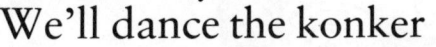

I've got a bonnet trimmed with blue,
Why don't you wear it? So I do.
When do you wear it? When I can,
When I go out with my young man.
My young man has gone to France,
To teach the ladies how to dance,
First the heel, and then the toe,
For that's the way the ladies go.

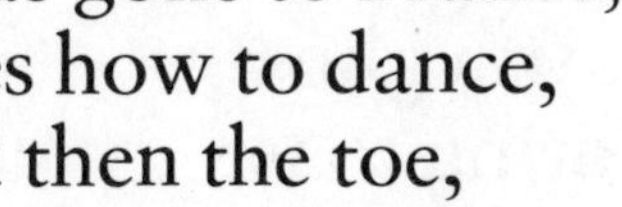

Mrs White got a fright
In the middle of the night,
Saw a ghost
Eating toast
Halfway up a lamp post.

Caroline, Caroline,
Dipped her nose in turpentine,
Turpentine made it shine,
What do you think of Caroline?

When Susie was a baby
A baby Susie was,
She went, 'Whaa, whaa, whaa whaa whaa.'

When Susie was a schoolgirl
A schoolgirl Susie was,
She went, 'Miss, Miss, I can't do this.'

When Susie was a teenager
A teenager Susie was,
She went, 'Ooh, aah, I lost my bra,
I left my knickers in my boyfriend's car.'

When Susie was a mother
A mother Susie was,
She went, 'Rock, rock, around the clock.'

When Susie was a grandmother
A grandmother Susie was,
She went, 'Knit, knit, you're a twit.'

When Susie was a dead
A dead Susie was,
She went . . . .

When Susie was a ghost
A ghost Susie was,
She went, '*Sho-oo-oo-oh-oh.*'

When Susie was a skeleton
A skeleton Susie was,
She went, 'Rattle rattle rattle rattle rattle.'

When Susie was an angel
An angel Susie was,
She went, 'Flap flap flap flap flap.'

My father came from Germany,
My mother came from Italy,
My sister came from the go-go shop
And the baby came from me me me.

My father works in the ABC,
My mother works in the bakery,
My sister works in the go-go shop
And the baby works with me me me.

My father likes to suck his pipe,
My mother likes to read a book,
My sister likes to shave her legs
And the baby follows me me me.

My father died in Germany,
My mother died in Italy,
My sister died in the go-go shop
And the baby died with me me me.

Blondie and Dagwood went to town,
Blondie bought a dressing-gown,
Dagwood bought a newspaper
And this is what it said:
Close your eyes and count to ten,
If you don't you'll hold the end.

My mother said, I never should,
Play with the gypsies in the wood.
If I did, she would say, naughty girl to disobey!
Tell your mother to hold her tongue —
She did the same when she was young.

Two, four, six, eight,
Mary at the cottage gate,
Eating cherries off a plate,
Two, four, six, eight.

Over the garden wall
I let the baby fall.
My mother came out
And gave me a clout
And knocked me over the wall,
The wall, the wall . . .

Mrs P
Mrs A
Mrs RRA
Mrs M
Mrs A
Mrs TTA
PARRAMATTA!

Mrs M
Mrs I
Mrs SSI
Mrs SSI
Mrs PPI
MISSISSIPPI!

Fatty and Skinny had a race
Up and down the fireplace.
Fatty stopped to feed his face —
Who do you think won the race?
S-K-I-N-N-Y spells skinny
And out you must go
Because I say so.

How many miles to Babylon?
Three score and ten, sir.
Can I get there by candlelight?
There and back again, sir.
Chip, chip, my little horse,
Chip, chip again, sir.
How many miles to Babylon?
Three score and ten, sir.

Stare, stare, like a bear,
Then you'll know me everywhere!

Sticky stare
Like a bear
I can see your underwear.
Maybe blue, maybe white,
Maybe covered in Vegemite.

Take a photo — it lasts longer.

Have a good look — the price goes up tomorrow.

Sticks and stones may break my bones
But names will never hurt me.

John is a mug
With a head like a jug
And a face like a rotten tomato!

Liar, liar,
Pants on fire!

Faker, faker,
You'll be eaten by the baker!

Tell tale tit, your tongue should be slit,
And all the little puppy dogs could have a little bit.

Think — it might be a new experience.

Thank you for your portrait,
I think it's very nice,
I put it in the attic
To scare away the mice.

Beg your pardon, Mrs Harden,
There's a chicken in your garden.

See you later, alligator,
Don't forget your toilet paper.

See you soon
You big baboon.
If you wish
Jellyfish.

Jump in the sea and pull a wave over your head.

Go hop, carrot top!
Drop dead, potato head!
Get real, banana peel!

Supersonic,
Idiotic
Brain-affected
Disconnected
Dumb-bell!

Your ears are like flowers.
Cauliflowers.

If you've got a minute, tell me all you know.

Your eyes shine
Like great pools of mud,
And your teeth are like stars —
They come out at night.

You're the south end of a north-bound camel.

Hinka, pinka,
I smell a stinka.

By egg or by bacon
I think you're mistaken.

Boys are strong, like King Kong.
Girls are stronger, they live longer.

Sealed With A Loving Kiss

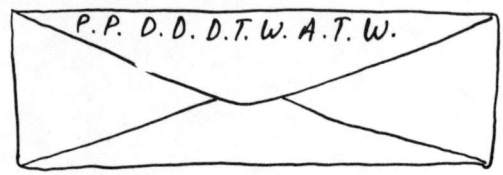

D-liver D-letter
D-sooner D-better
D-slower D-letter
D-sadder D-getter.

Postman, postman don't delay
Do the Watusi all the way.

Train Tracks

A ship in a fog.

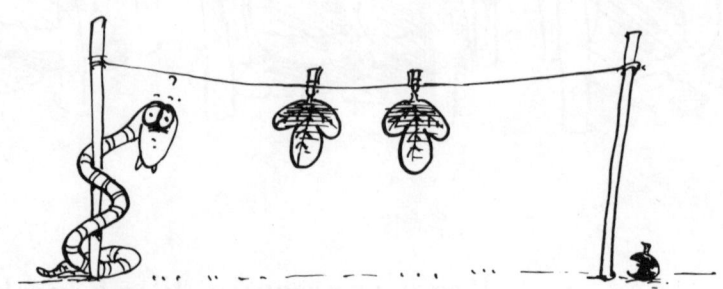

Adam and Eve's washing.

Never B#
Never B♭
Always B♮

G U R A Q T!
I N V U!

Just a few lines about myself.

JUNE

'Yellow River' by I. P. Daily.

Life is like a deck of cards:

 when you're in love

 when you're engaged

 when you're married

 when you're dead.

A piece of glass will make you pass.
A rusty nail will make you fail.

True friends are like diamonds,
Precious and rare,
False friends are like autumn leaves,
Found everywhere.

Sawdust makes wood
Wood makes paper
Paper makes books
Books make brains.

If you want a cool surprise
Pull the chain before you rise.

Pleasant dreams and sweet repose,
If you lie on your back you won't squash your nose.

Good night,
Sweet repose,
Hope the fleas don't bite your toes.

If this book should chance to roam
And you should chance to find it,
Box its ears and send it home —
No need for you to mind it.

Black is the raven, black is the rook,
Blackest is the one who steals this book.

For adults

Like *Far Out, Brussel Sprout!* (Melbourne, Oxford University Press, 1983), this book offers a sampling from the rich storehouse of children's folklore. The rhymes, games and jokes come from every State in Australia, and almost all are found in more than one State. However, the bulk of the material was collected from, or submitted by, children in Victoria.

For those interested in the role of adults *vis-à-vis* this lore, there is a short discussion at the end of *Far Out, Brussel Sprout*. There are also many books, mostly American and British, which contain similar material from children in those countries, as well as discussion of the nature and significance of this fundamental and enduring feature of children's culture. The following titles provide further readings of and about Australian children's folklore.

DAVEY, G. *Folklore and the Enculturation of Young Immigrant Children in Melbourne.* Unpublished M.Ed thesis, Melbourne, Monash University, 1983.

FACTOR, J. *Childhood and Children's Culture.* Melbourne, Australian Children's Television Foundation, 1985.

HOPE, C. *Themes from the Playground.* Melbourne, Thomas Nelson Australia, 1984.

INSTITUTE OF EARLY CHILDHOOD DEVELOPMENT. *Australian Children's Folklore Newsletter.* vol. 1, no. 1 –, Melbourne, 1981.

LINDSAY, P. L. and PALMER, D. *Playground Game Characteristics of Brisbane Primary School Children.* Canberra, Australian Government Publishing Service, 1981.

LOWENSTEIN, W. *Shocking, Shocking, Shocking: The Improper Play Rhymes of Australian Children.* Melbourne, Fish & Chip Press, 1974.

RAMSHAW, J. (ed.). *Folklore in Australia*. Paddington Queensland, Australian Folk Trust, 1985.

TURNER, I., FACTOR, J. and LOWENSTEIN, W. *Cinderella Dressed in Yella*. Melbourne, Heinemann Australia, 1982.

RAMSHAW, L. (ed.), *Folklore in Australia*, Paddington Queensland, Australian Folk Trust, 1983.

SEEBA, I., FACTOR, J. and LOWENSTEIN, W. *Claimed a Dream in Yada*, Melbourne, Hyland House, Alistairs, 1982.